27 HABITS TO HAPPINESS

Rev. Dr. Timmy Lundale Sykes

"Happiness Comes From

Being Obedient To God!"

To God my Heavenly Father, Jesus Christ my Savior, and the Holy Spirit my Comforter...

To all the people who have helped me become...

The folks who raised me— Dad, *Joseph Lewis Sykes, Mom, *Joyce Marie Foreman-Sykes, and my vast immediate and extended family,

My circle of strong men, women, boys, and girls whom God allowed me to serve as their Pastor...

Pilgrim Rock Missionary Baptist Church, Chattanooga, TN (Sister Arma Jean Broomfield & the late Deacon William Smith, Sr.), Beyond Words Baptist Church, Jefferson, GA., Deacon Chris & Valerie Randolph, Brother Marvin & Sister Erica Johnson, Rev. Annie Dukes, Rev. Mike Holcomb, Rev. Lavida Daniels, Gethsemane Missionary Baptist Church, Galveston, TX, Rev. Robert Simpson, Sister Lillian McGrew, Sister Barbara Kelly, Sister Pat Toliver, Sister Dolores Johnson, Sister Darlene Randle, each and every member of all three churches, including members of Mount Moriah Missionary Baptist Church, Galveston, TX, whom ALL, always Spiritually lifted me up, as I served as their Pastor.

My loyal and dedicated Pastors;
****Dr. Ernest L. Gates, *Dr. Melvin Jordan, *Dr. Nathaniel Carter, Sr., (*All resting with Lord in Heaven*)***

My current Pastor, Dr. Ternae T. Jordan, Sr.

My on-line publishing staff at Kindle Direct Publishing, who continue to make me proud **as a publishing partner.**

To the loves of my life:

Naomi, Tyler, Thomas, and Zion, my most precious children, who are my reasons for being, and finally, Deshunira, my Beloved wife, who always promised me an interesting love life journey.

La Marque, TX

Printed in the United States of America

First Printing, September 2022

ISBN: 9798353885689
Out of Sykes Publishing
Send email to: pastorsykes@gmail.com

Daily habits

The following daily habits may help you achieve more happiness in your life.

1. Smile

You tend to smile when you are happy. But it is actually a two-way street.

We smile because we're happy and smiling causes the brain to release dopamine, which makes us happier.

While not completely foolproof, researchers have found that the link between smiling and happiness could be attributed to the "facial feedback hypothesis," where facial expressions may have a modest influence on emotions.

That does not mean you have to go around with a fake smile plastered on your face all the time. But the next time you find yourself feeling low, crack a smile and see what happens. Or try starting each morning by smiling at yourself in the mirror.

2. Exercise

Exercise is not just for your body. Regular exercise can help reduce stress, feelings of anxiety, and symptoms of depression while boosting self-esteem and happiness.

Even a small amount of physical activity can make a difference. You don't have to train for a triathlon or scale a cliff — unless that's what makes you happy, of course.

The trick is to not overexert yourself. If you suddenly throw yourself into a strenuous routine, you may just end up frustrated (and sore).

Consider these exercise starters:

- Take a walk around the block every night after dinner.
- Sign up for a beginner's class in yoga or tai chi.
- Start your day with 5 minutes of stretching.

Remind yourself of any fun activities you once enjoyed but that have fallen by the wayside. Or you could consider starting activities you always wanted to try, such as golf, bowling, or dancing.

3. Get plenty of sleep

Most adults need at least 7 hours of sleep every night. If you find yourself fighting the urge to nap during the day or just generally feel like you are in a fog, your body may be telling you it needs more rest.

No matter how much our modern society steers us toward less sleep, we know that adequate sleep is vital to good health, brain function, and emotional well-being. Getting enough sleep also reduces your risk Trusted Source of developing certain chronic illnesses, such as heart disease, depression, and diabetes.

Here are a few tips to help you build a better sleep routine:

- Write down how many hours of sleep you get each night and how rested you feel. After a week, you should have a better idea how you are doing. You can also try using an app to track your sleep.
- Go to bed and wake up at the same time every day, including on weekends.

- Reserve the hour before bed as quiet time. Take a bath, read, or do something relaxing. Avoid heavy eating and drinking.
- Keep your bedroom dark, cool, and quiet.
- Invest in some good bedding.
- If you have to take a nap, try limiting it to 20 minutes.

If you consistently have problems sleeping, consider talking with a doctor. You may have a sleep disorder that requires treatment.

4. Eat with mood in mind

You may already know that your food choices have an impact on your overall physical health. But some foods can also affect your state of mind.

For example:

- **Carbohydrates** release serotonin, a "feel good" hormone. Just keep simple carbs — foods high in sugar and starch — to a minimum because that energy surge is short, and you will crash. Choosing complex carbs, such as vegetables, beans, and whole grains, can help you avoid a crash while still providing serotonin.
- **Lean meat, poultry, legumes, and dairy** are high in protein. Protein-rich foods release dopamine and norepinephrine, which boost energy and concentration.
- **Omega-3 fatty acids**, such as those found in fatty fish, have been found to have anti-inflammatory

effects that extend to your overall brain health. If you do not eat fish, you might consider talking with a doctor about possible supplementation.

- **Highly processed or deep-fried foods** tend to leave you feeling down and so will skipping meals.

If you want to eat with your mood in mind, consider starting with making one food choice for your mood each day.

For example, swap a big, sweet breakfast pastry for some Greek yogurt with fruit. You will still satisfy your sweet tooth, and the protein will help you avoid a midmorning energy crash. Consider adding in a new food swap each week.

5. Practice gratitude

Simply being grateful can give your mood a big boost, among other benefits. For example, a two-part study found that practicing gratitude can have a significant impact on feelings of hope and happiness.

You might try starting each day by acknowledging one thing for which you are grateful. You can do this while you are brushing your teeth or just waiting for that snoozed alarm to go off.

As you go about your day, consider keeping an eye out for pleasant things in your life. They can be big things, such as knowing that someone loves you or getting a well-deserved promotion.

But they can also be little things, such as a co-worker who offered you a cup of coffee or the neighbor who waved to you. Maybe it could even just be the warmth of the sun on your skin.

With a little practice, you may even become more aware of all the positive things around you.

6. Give a compliment

Research shows that performing acts of kindness may also help promote your overall well-being.

Giving a sincere compliment is a quick, easy way to brighten someone's day while giving your own happiness a boost.

Catch the person's eye and say it with a smile so they know you mean it. You might be surprised by how good it makes you feel.

If you want to offer someone a compliment on their physical appearance, make sure to do it in a respectful way.

7. Breathe deeply

You are tense, your shoulders are tight, and you feel as though you just might "lose it." We all know that feeling.

Instinct may tell you to take a long, deep breath to calm yourself down.

Turns out, that instinct is a good one. Research supports the fact that slow breathing and deep breathing exercises can help reduce stress.

The next time you feel stressed or are at your wit's end, work through these steps:

1. Close your eyes. Try to envision a happy memory or beautiful place.
2. Take a slow, deep breath in through your nose.
3. Slowly breathe out through your mouth or nose.
4. Repeat this process several times until you start to feel yourself calm down.

If you are having a hard time taking slow, deliberate breaths, try counting to 5 in your head with each inhale and exhale.

8. Acknowledge the unhappy moments

A positive attitude is generally a good thing, but bad things happen to everyone. It is just part of life.

If you get some bad news, make a mistake, or just feel like you're in a funk, don't try to pretend you're happy.

Acknowledge the feeling of unhappiness, letting yourself experience it for a moment. Then shift your focus toward what made you feel this way and what it might take to recover.

Would a deep breathing exercise help? A long walk outside? Talking it over with someone?

Let the moment pass and take care of yourself. Remember, no one's happy all the time.

9. Keep a journal

A journal is a good way to organize your thoughts, analyze your feelings, and make plans. And you do not have to be a literary genius or write volumes to benefit.

It can be as simple as jotting down a few thoughts before you go to bed. If putting certain things in writing makes you nervous, you can always shred it when you have finished. It is the process that counts.

Not sure what to do with all the feelings that end up on the page? Our guide to organizing your feelings may help.

10. Face stress head-on

Life is full of stressors, and it is impossible to avoid all of them.

There is no need to. Stress isn't always harmful, and we can even change our attitudes about stress. Sometimes, there is an upside to stress.

For those stressors you cannot avoid, remind yourself that everyone has stress — there is no reason to think it is all on you. And chances are, you are stronger than you might think you are.

Instead of letting yourself get overwhelmed, try to address the stressor head-on. This might mean starting an uncomfortable conversation or putting in some extra work, but the sooner you confront it, the sooner the pit in your stomach may start to shrink.

11. Avoid comparing yourself to others

Whether it happens on social media, at work, or even at a yoga class, it's easy to fall into a place where you're comparing yourself to others. The result? You may experience more discontent, lower self-esteem, and even depression and anxiety.

It can take practice to stop comparing yourself to others, but it's worth it for the benefit of having your inner peace and happiness.

You can start with some of the other tips on this list that can help draw your attention inward to yourself, such as deep breathing and journaling. You may also consider talking with a therapist for perspective.

Weekly habits

The following tips include weekly habits that may help you feel happier.

12. Declutter

Decluttering sounds like a big project but setting aside just 20 minutes a week can have a big impact.

What can you do in 20 minutes? Lots.

Set a timer on your phone and take 15 minutes to tidy up a specific area of one room — say, your closet or that out-of-control junk drawer. Put everything in its place and toss or give away any extra clutter that is not serving you anymore.

Keep a designated box for giveaways to make things a little easier (and avoid creating more clutter).

Use the remaining 5 minutes to do a quick walk through your living space, putting away whatever stray items end up in your path.

You can do this trick once a week, once a day, or anytime you feel like your space is getting out of control.

13. See friends

Humans are largely considered social beings, and while the research is mixed on how exactly socialization impacts happiness, the consensus is that having social relationships can make us happy.

Who do you miss? Reach out to them. Make a date to get together or simply have a long phone chat.

In adulthood, it can feel next to impossible to make new friends. But it is not about how many friends you have. It is about having meaningful relationships — even if it is just with one or two people.

Try getting involved in a local volunteer group or taking a class. Both can help connect you with like-minded people in your area. And it is likely they're looking for friends, too.

Companionship does not have to be limited to other humans. Pets can offer similar benefits, according to multiple studies.

Love animals but cannot have a pet? Consider volunteering at a local animal shelter to make some new friends — both human and animal.

14. Plan your week

Feel like you are flailing about? Try sitting down at the end of every week and making a basic list for the following week.

Even if you do not stick to the plan, blocking out time where you can do laundry, go grocery shopping, or tackle projects at work can help quiet your mind.

You can get a fancy planner or app, but even a sticky note on your computer or piece of scrap paper in your pocket can do the job.

15. Ditch your phone

Unplug. Really.

There's mounting evidence to support the fact that excessive phone use can lead to changes in the brain and impact your mood, with one review even revealing more serious cognitive and emotional changes in adolescents and young adults.

Turn off all the electronics and put those earbuds away for at least 1 hour once a week. They will still be there for you later if you want them.

If you have not unplugged in a while, you might be surprised at the difference it makes. Let your mind wander free for a change. Read. Meditate. Take a walk and pay attention to your surroundings. Be sociable. Or be alone. Just be.

Sound too daunting? Try unplugging for a shorter amount of time several times a week.

16. Get into nature

Spending 30 minutes or more a week in green spaces can help lower blood pressure and the chances of developing depression, according to one study Trusted Source.

Your green space could be anything such as your neighborhood park, your own backyard, or a rooftop garden — anywhere you can appreciate and enjoy nature and fresh air.

Better yet, add some outdoor exercise into the mix for extra benefit. The same aforementioned study found that people who spent time in green spaces were also more likely to exercise more often and for longer each time.

17. Explore meditation

There are many methods of meditation to explore. They can involve movement, focus, spirituality, or a combination of all three.

Meditation does not have to be complicated. It can be as simple as sitting quietly with your own thoughts for 5 minutes. Even the deep breathing exercises mentioned earlier can serve as a form of meditation.

18. Consider therapy

We are certainly happier when we learn how to cope with obstacles. When you are faced with a problem, think about what got you through something similar in the past. Would it work here? What else can you try?

If you feel like you are hitting a brick wall, consider speaking with a mental health professional like a therapist on a weekly basis. You don't need to have a diagnosed mental health condition or overwhelming crisis to seek therapy.

Mental health professionals are trained to help people improve coping skills. Plus, there is no obligation to continue once you start.

Even just a few sessions can help you add some new goodies to your emotional toolbox.

Worried about the cost? It is possible to afford therapy on any budget.

19. Find a self-care ritual

It's easy to neglect self-care in a fast-paced world. But trying to find time to nurture yourself as much as you can is important in supporting your body's responsibilities of carrying your thoughts, passions, and spirit through this world.

Maybe it's unwinding your workweek with a long, hot bath. Or it may be adopting a skin care routine that makes you feel indulgent. Or it could be simply setting aside a night to put on your softest jammies and watch a movie from start to finish.

Whatever it is, be available for it. Put it in your planner if you must but try to make it a priority do it.

Monthly habits

You might want to give these monthly habits to improve your happiness a try.

20. Give back

If you find that giving daily compliments provides a needed boost to your mood, consider making a monthly routine of giving back on a larger scale.

Maybe that's helping out at a food bank on the third weekend of every month or offering to watch your friend's kids one night per month.

21. Take yourself out

No one to go out with? Well, what rule says you cannot go out alone?

Consider going to your favorite restaurant, taking in a movie, or going on that trip you have always dreamed of.

Even if you're a social butterfly, spending some deliberate time alone can help you reconnect with the activities that truly make you happy.

22. Create a thought list

You arrive for an appointment with 10 minutes to spare. What do you do with that time? Pick up your cell phone to scroll through social media? Worry about the busy week you have ahead of you?

Trying to take control of your thoughts during these brief windows of time can offer benefits.

At the start of each month, make a short list of happy memories or things you're looking forward to on a small piece of paper or on your phone.

When you find yourself waiting for a ride, standing in line at the grocery store, or just with a few minutes to kill, break out the list. You can even use it when you are just generally feeling down and need to change up your thoughts.

Yearly habits

Try following habits once a year or more to reflect and plan for happiness.

23. Take time to reflect

While the start of a new year is a good time to stop and take inventory of your life, you can set up yearly habits at any point in the year. Try setting aside some time to catch up with yourself the way you would with an old friend:

- How are you doing?
- What have you been up to?
- Are you happier than you were a year ago?

But try to avoid judging yourself too harshly for your answers. You have made it to another year, and that is a reason to celebrate.

If you find that your mood has not improved much over the last year, consider talking with a doctor or mental health professional. You might be dealing with depression or even an underlying physical condition that's affecting your mood.

24. Reevaluate your goals

People change, so try thinking about where you are heading and consider if that is still where you want to go. There is no shame in changing your plans.

Let go of any goals that no longer serve you, even if they sound nice on paper.

25. Take care of your body

You have likely heard this before, including several times in this article. Your physical and mental health are closely intertwined.

As you build habits to improve your happiness, it is important to follow up with routine appointments to help take care your body, such as:

- seeing a primary care physician for an annual physical
- discussing and addressing any chronic health conditions with a healthcare professional and seeing recommended specialists if needed
- seeing a dentist for an oral cleaning and dental exam, and follow up as recommended
- getting your vision checked

26. Let go of grudges

This can often be easier said than done. But remembering that you are not necessarily doing it for another person or other people may help you be more open to beginning the process.

Sometimes, offering forgiveness or dropping a grudge is more about self-care than compassion for others.

Take stock of your relationships with others. Are you harboring any resentment or ill will toward someone? If so, consider reaching out to them in an effort to bury the hatchet.

This does not have to be a reconciliation. You may just need to end the relationship and move on.

If reaching out is not an option, try getting your feelings out in a letter. You do not even have to send it to them. Just getting your feelings out of your mind and into the world can be freeing. You can even shred the letter afterward if you want to.

27. Plan a trip

With an ever-hectic schedule, sometimes it is easy to forget to schedule something else that is crucial to your well-being: time off. You can reap even more benefits by planning a trip, whether it is close to home or somewhere further away.

What's more, research also backs both the mental *and* physical benefits of taking that much-needed vacation. In one such study, researchers looked at stress and heart rate as it relates to taking a vacation. They found that not only did the vacation itself reduce stress, but the weeks leading up to that planned trip had similar effects.

The search for happiness is not a new one. When you end the day wishing you could just feel happier, you are not alone. It is easy to think that you will be happy once you reach a certain milestone. Maybe it's when your retirement is fully funded, you graduate college, or get married.

Or perhaps you think when your kids are finally potty trained, you'll feel it. Happiness. Unfortunately, once your last child is potty trained, the happiness train does not just pull in. Then you pick another day. Another time when you will be happy.

Thankfully you don't have to wait until that elusive day to feel happier. You can start today by building habits into your daily routine that can help you feel happy, no matter your life circumstances. Try doing these habits on a daily basis for a few months and see if they make a difference.

"Hug harder. Laugh louder. Smile bigger. Love longer." ~Unknown

Did you ever have it all mixed up?

Happiness, I mean. I once thought that a university degree and good grades would make me happy. I thought that traveling the world would leave me feeling fulfilled. I thought that moving abroad and getting that top-notch job would make me satisfied and content.

They all did, but only for a while. They always came with an expiration date.

Finally, I had to stop and ask myself, “If I’m not able to be truly happy now, will I ever be?” If I could not appreciate everything I *already* had in my life, would more really be the answer?

No!

Then I thought, “If happiness is what I want, why not just go there directly?”

So, I did. I stopped putting it on hold. I stopped allowing external circumstances to dictate how I felt. And I stopped relying on illusionary destinations of promised happiness and bliss.

What I realized is that happiness does not happen by chance–it happens by *choice*. It is a skill that anyone can develop with the right habits.

Claim Your Happiness Once And For All

Not being in charge of your happiness is frustrating. Relying on external events and circumstances to be in a certain way in order to feel good is a recipe for misery. Because, when life does not go as planned or things fall apart, so does our happiness.

Happiness is not about having all the pieces in place. It is not about having a problem-free life or reaching a certain goal or objective. Instead, it is about being able to enjoy where you are, no matter what.

Do not leave your happiness to chance. Choose to claim it. Live the life you deserve to live.

Modern society conditions us to believe that happiness is a destination we arrive at: the promotion that will wash away all our problems, the new car that will make us feel good, the freedom we will obtain from leaving a 9–5.

So, we now live with this idea: "When X happens, I'll be happy."

I lived the entirety of the past decade cultivating this toxic mentality and it affected every major decision I made in my life. I was always chasing the next grandiose thing, in constant pursuit of happiness, never truly indulging in the fullness of what I already had.

Despite having it all — the new job in New York, the close-knit friends, the jet-setter lifestyle — I was unhappy, and I didn't know why.

So, I reverted back to Christian Biblical teachings and arrived at the realization that happiness is not a distant island we must travel to, happiness is a place we already live in because happiness is found within us.

Happiness a deep-rooted rose of contentment that you carry with you everywhere you go — and you are the one who chooses whether or not to water it every morning upon waking up.

Happiness exists right here, right now.

If you fail to appreciate this sentiment and continue to chase the big elusive dream of a distant happy future, then you will never experience the self-worth and contentment that can be found in this present moment.

Our sole objective is to turn our gaze inward and find all the barriers within ourselves that we have unconsciously built to bury that happiness beneath our sight. How do we do that? We form new habits that cast away the shadows and allow us to see the light again.

Happy people understand the one fundamental truth of life: What you focus on expands. So, if you are constantly engaging with depressing, self-critical, or negative thoughts, well then guess what? Your life experience will reflect those very thoughts you are giving your attention to.

And that's exactly why happy people practice gratitude.

Every day, they actively divert their attention to what they already have instead of what they lack. They express gratitude for what they are working on instead of lamenting over what they have not been able to achieve yet. And that's how opportunities flow their way.

People with a fixed mindset do not deal well with challenges and everything they do is driven with the intention of bolstering their ego. But not happy people; they focus on their personal development instead. They practice surrender, embrace failure, and seek opportunities to learn something new.

Seek transcendence, not ego. Seek unity, not individuality. Seek education, not entertainment. Seek effort, not 'hacks.' All these are qualities that cultivate a rich growth mindset.

Choosing to be grateful, choosing to be kind, to be available for what you love, to stay positive, to slow down, to exercise, and seek growth — all these are habits within your control.

In any given situation, always choose to focus on what is within your control. Anything else you give your energy and attention to strips away your power.

You have to make an effort to be happy.

No one wakes up feeling happy every day, but happy people do their best to frame their mornings with positivity. They work harder at it than anyone else because they recognize that happiness takes inner-work and effort.

They constantly reflect and evaluate, monitor, and explore. And wherever they go, they carry the twenty-seven habits listed in this book with them; because they know that happiness is not a destination you arrive at, **happiness is the way!**

Feed your brain with things that give you insight, empowerment, and motivation. Even reading about authentic happiness makes you happier.

In short, we tend to have unreasonable expectations. The difference between what we feel entitled to and what we actually get is the source of much misery.

Accept life in its entirety; stop thinking in terms of what should be and accept what is. When you live without entitlement, every good thing becomes a wonderful surprise. Even better, expecting nothing means never being disappointed.

Conclusion

At the end of the day, dreadful things will happen to you. You will have highs, lows, and lots of mediums in your life. You are only human, just like everybody else.

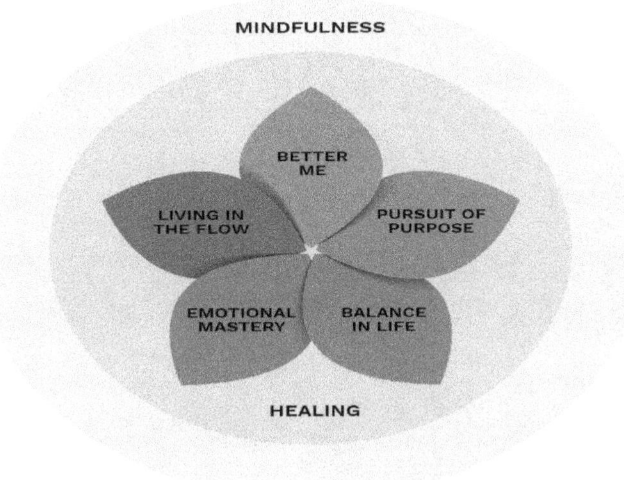

Never depend on anyone to bring happiness to you! Happiness is self-inflicted and comes from within! It is given by God to those that are obedient to His Will!

Thanks for your support in this purchase of this book!

May God Bless You Always!

Dr. Timmy Lundale Sykes

www.ingramcontent.com/pod-product-compliance
Lightning Source LLC
LaVergne TN
LVHW010514160826
845677LV00012B/2855

* 9 7 9 8 3 5 3 8 8 5 6 8 9 *